W9-BSJ-006

DESESPERANTO

MARILYN HACKER

DESESPERANTO

Poems 1999–2002

W. W. NORTON & COMPANY

New York · London

For information about permission to reproduce selections from this book, write to
Permissions, W. W. Norton & Company, Inc., 500 Fifth Avenue, New York, NY 10110

Manufacturing by The Courier Companies, Inc.
Book design by Charlotte Staub
Production manager: Anna Oler

Library of Congress Cataloging-in-Publication Data

Hacker, Marilyn, 1942–
Desesperanto : poems, 1999–2002 / by Marilyn Hacker. —1st ed.
p. cm.
ISBN 0-393-05418-7 (hardcover)
I. Title.
PS3558.A28 D47 2003
811'.54—dc21

2002154390

W. W. Norton & Company, Inc., 500 Fifth Avenue, New York, N.Y. 10110
www.wwnorton.com

W. W. Norton & Company Ltd., Castle House, 75/76 Wells Street,
London W1T 3QT

1 2 3 4 5 6 7 8 9 0

for Mavis Gallant

CONTENTS

ITINERANTS

DESESPERANTO

ACKNOWLEDGMENTS

Grateful acknowledgment is given to the journals in which poems in this book originally appeared: *The Crab Orchard Review; The Forward; The Gay and Lesbian Review; The Kenyon Review; The London Magazine; The Massachusetts Review; Metre; The New England Review; New Letters; The Paris Review; Parnassus; Pequod; Ploughshares; PN Review; Poetry International; Poetry London; Prairie Schooner; The Princeton Library Chronicle; The Progressive; Ratapallax; The Seattle Review; TriQuarterly; Upstairs at Duroc; Van Gogh's Ear; The Women's Review of Books; The Yale Review.*

"Grief" and "Respite in a Minor Key" first appeared in *The Nation*

"Desesperanto," "Essay on Departure," and "Sonnet on a Line by Vénus Khoury-Ghata" first appeared in *Poetry*

"Explication de texte" received the Smart Family Foundation Award from *The Yale Review* in 2001

DESESPERANTO

Elegy for a Soldier

June Jordan, 1936–2002

I.

The city where I knew you was swift.
A lover cabbed to Brooklyn
(broke, but so what) after the night shift
in a Second Avenue
diner. The lover was a Quaker,
a poet, an anti-war
activist. Was blonde, was twenty-four.
Wet snow fell on the access
road to the Manhattan Bridge. I was
neither lover, slept uptown.
But the arteries, streetlights, headlines,
phonelines, feminine plural
links ran silver through the night city
as dawn and the yellow cab
passed on the frost-blurred bridge, headed for
that day's last or first coffee.

The city where I knew you was rich
in bookshops, potlucks, ad hoc
debates, demos, parades and picnics.
There were walks I liked to take.
I was on good terms with two rivers.
You turned, burned, flame-wheel of words
lighting the page, good neighbor on your
homely street in Park Slope, whose
Russian zaydes, Jamaican grocers,
dyke vegetarians, young

gifted everyone, claimed some changes
—at least a new food co-op.
In the laundromat, ordinary
women talked revolution.
We knew we wouldn't live forever
but it seemed as if we could.

The city where I knew you was yours
and mine by birthright: Harlem,
the Bronx. Separately we left it
and came separately back.
There's no afterlife for dialogue,
divergences we never
teased apart to weave back together.
Death slams down in the midst of
all your unfinished conversations.
Whom do I address when I
address you, larger than life as you
always were, not alive now?
Words are not you, poems are not you,
ashes on the Pacific
tide, you least of all. I talk to my-
self to keep the line open.

The city where I knew you is gone.
Pink icing roses spelled out
PASSION on a book-shaped chocolate cake.
The bookshop's a sushi bar
now, and PASSION is long out of print.
Would you know the changed street that
cab swerved down toward you through cold white mist?
We have a Republican
mayor. Threats keep citizens in line:

anthrax; suicide attacks.
A scar festers where towers once were;
dissent festers unexpressed.
You are dead of a woman's disease.
Who gets to choose what battle
takes her down? Down to the ocean, friends
mourn you, with no time to mourn.

II.

You, who stood alone in the tall bay window
of a Brooklyn brownstone, conjuring morning
with free-flying words, knew the power, terror
in words, in flying;

knew the high of solitude while the early
light prowled Seventh Avenue, lupine, hungry
like you, your spoils raisins and almonds, ballpoint
pen, yellow foolscap.

You, who stood alone in your courage, never
hesitant to underline the connections
(between rape, exclusion and occupation . . .)
and separations

were alone and were not alone when morning
blotted the last spark of you out, around you
voices you no longer had voice to answer,
eyes you were blind to.

All your loves were singular: you scorned labels.
Claimed *black*; *woman*, and for the rest eluded
limits, quicksilver (Caribbean), staked out
self-definition.

Now your death, as if it were "yours": your house, your
dog, your friends, your son, your serial lovers.
Death's not "yours," what's yours are a thousand poems
alive on paper,

in the present tense of a thousand students'
active gaze at printed pages and blank ones
which you gave permission to blacken into
outrage and passion.

You, at once an optimist, a Cassandra,
Lilith in the wilderness of her lyric,
were a black American, born in Harlem,
citizen soldier

If you had to die—and I don't admit it—
who dared "What if, each time they kill a black man /
we kill a cop?" couldn't you take down with you
a few prime villains

in the capitol, who are also mortal?
June, you should be living, the states are bleeding.
Leaden words like "Homeland" translate abandoned
dissident discourse.

Twenty years ago, you denounced the war crimes
still in progress now, as Jenin, Ramallah
dominate, then disappear from the headlines.
Palestine: your war.

"To each nation, its Jews," wrote Primo Levi.
"Palestinians are Jews to Israelis."
Afterwards, he died in despair, or so we
infer, despairing.

To each nation its Jews, its blacks, its Arabs,
Palestinians, immigrants, its women.
From each nation, its poets: Mahmoud Darwish,
Kavanagh, Sháhid

(who, beloved witness for silenced Kashmir,
cautioned, shift the accent, and he was "martyr"),
Audre Lorde, Neruda, Amichai, Senghor,
and you, June Jordan.

VENDANGES

Crepuscule with Muriel

Instead of a cup of tea, instead of a milk-
silk whelk of a cup, of a cup of nearly six
o'clock teatime, cup of a stumbling block,
cup of an afternoon unredeemed by talk,
cup of a cut brown loaf, of a slice, a lack
of butter, blueberry jam that's almost black,
instead of tannin seeping into the cracks
of a pot, the void of an hour seeps out, infects
the slit of a cut I haven't the wit to fix
with a surgeon's needle threaded with fine-gauge silk
as a key would thread the cylinder of a lock.
But no key threads the cylinder of the lock.
Late afternoon light, transitory, licks
the place of the absent cup with its rough tongue, flicks
itself out beneath the wheel's revolving spoke.
Taut thought's gone, with a blink of attention, slack,
a vision of "death and distance in the mix"
(she lost her words and how did she get them back
when the corridor of a day was a lurching deck?
The dream-life logic encodes in nervous tics
she translated to a syntax which connects
intense and unfashionable politics
with morning coffee, Hudson sunsets, sex;
then the short-circuit of the final stroke,
the end toward which all lines looped out, then broke).
What a gaze out the window interjects:
on the southeast corner, a black Lab balks,
tugged as the light clicks green toward a late-day walk
by a plump brown girl in a purple anorak.
The Bronx-bound local comes rumbling up the tracks

out of the tunnel, over west Harlem blocks
whose windows gleam on the animal warmth of bricks
rouged by the fluvial light of six o'clock.

Days of 1999

One unexceptional bright afternoon
in August, coming from the rose garden
secreted behind the rue Villehardouin,
I thought, fleet, furtive, if I lived alone
I could stay here
                              and pushed the thought away
as firmly and unlikely as *Might rain
later* because I wanted just to choose
and I had chosen, more than cobblestones
and arbors, more than the benediction
of new loaves' scent blown from the bakery,
the benediction of the late white rose,
more than the blank page of the cloudless sky,
to honor choice, reflecting on it daily
but even as the thought diminished on
a wave of warm bread and the holiday
banter of children with no homework to do
a choice I never made was made for me
in another mind, another country
I thought I had some claim to, which I knew
not at all, as that warm wave let me drift
with no anticipating harbor left.
Spring showers wash the hidden rose garden;
an evening's bread is rising in an oven:
the afternoon's word resonates *alone*
as a sky, mother-and-fatherless
in its gray and quotidian distress
blurts the repeated questions of the rain.

Embittered Elegy

i.m. Matthew Shepard and Dr. Barnett Slepian

Sheltered by womanhood and middle age
from their opinionated ignorance
since I'm their teacher, since they're my students,
I try to wedge bars of their local cage
open. . . . But what they're freed to voice is rage
against every adjacent difference.
The week the boy froze on the barbed-wire fence
a strapping senior roasted "men in drag":
bad attitude, grotesque, arrogant, ugly.
And if some skinny gay kid, black like him
(as Matthew and his torturers all were white)
made an inopportune advance one night,
what would be his righteous masculine
response? Flagellate and crucify?

Who's keen to flagellate and crucify?
The sleek umber young man was more complex
than his predictable gender-and-sex
prejudices. What idea or fantasy
was fleshed for him in Thom Gunn's elegies?
And the tall blonde girl, her long neck's
chignon a dancer's, in what context
was it revealed to her that *feminazi*
was the word for other young women who
railed against a certain status quo—
jealous, of course, deserving to be beaten?
Did she think I might imagine my own arm-bone
splinter as grinning frat boys knocked me down
while I read (with a teacher's distance) what she'd written?

While I read (with a teacher's distance) what she'd written
—her *sturmbannführerin*: a lesbian Jew—
I wondered what violence she'd been witness to
or suffered, that she had, or had not, forgotten,
but could not name, that prompted her to threaten
anyone who'd try to tell her, "you
don't have to take that shit." But I withdrew;
something heavier than indifference set in
and neither her fresh grace nor her obvious
pain provided me with the right questions.
In my windowless and anonymous
office painted institutional green, her
awkward plea hid in a trial sestina
behind a slur devised by "right-wing Christians."

Behind a slur devised by "right-wing Christians"
the battered boy hangs naked on barbed wire;
a picture window shatters in sniper fire:
the obstetrician who performed abortions
bleeds into Sabbath bread.
                              (That week's distortions
which Pizza Hut evangelists inspired
featured angelic embryos, martyred
by selfish women with degenerate notions.)
In a bare-walled projection-booth-sized room,
the students pass the week's assignment out.
A pile grows on my desk, page upon page,
in which, against the odds, may be a poem,
instead of calumnies from which I'm not
sheltered by womanhood and middle age.

English 182

Of fourteen students in "American Women
Poets of the 20th Century,"
(mostly Italian daughters of White Flight)
only one had ever taken
another course where she'd read poetry.
Meter, Modernism, metaphor:
words from some short-wave broadcast, late at night. . . .
Millay was "much too intellectual,"
Neither "Sappho" nor "Sacco" raised a brow.
We were a little vague on World War II.
We hadn't ever heard of Emmett Till.
I wanted recognition, someone's eyes
widening, a smile, complicity. . . .
Two late afternoons a week: the fall
fell, the basement window narrowed light.
I fixed on the one black student: might she surprise
both of us with some discovery,
not stare back blankly when I called on her
and say "I haven't done the reading"? She
was large and shy; framed her thoughts awkwardly,
but scrupulous B's were what she earned
on homework, until term's end, when she turned
in a mostly plagiarized term paper
on Plath (whose critics more unerringly
tempt plagiarists than her biographers
tempt suicide). When she saw her grade: a C
(out of wrong-headed generosity),
she stumbled from the classroom, stayed away
for twenty minutes, came back, took her seat
red-eyed, and sat there ostentatiously

not opening the text-anthology
where I'd assigned three poems by Audre Lorde.
Of course I called on her. Firmly, she said
"My book's not open."—as if she were bored.
At six, when I dismissed the class, she stayed
behind, and burst in tears—about her grade.
She was a graduating senior, and
an English major; she had worked so hard
on that paper, and she wasn't used
to getting low grades. (Everything she'd done
earlier, ungrammatical, handwritten
and tentatively spelled had been her own.)
Three others of her classmates had produced
plagiarized papers   she wasn't unique.
But there she'd sat, glaring dully at me
while I discussed black women's poetry
refusing to make eye contact or speak
as if her silence were an accident,
as if I didn't know what failure meant.

Days of 1967

Leaf-mulch, wood-smoke odor of Lapsang Souchong:
afternoons with Bill, unemployed, the Fillmore
full of run-down flats you could rent for nothing.
Unfinished paintings

covered peeling wallpaper, crumbling plaster.
He mapped out interior decoration:
It would be a gallery, our salon rival
Mme de Staël's.

Sutter Street was close enough to Perine Place
for impromptu visits (no phone) and we were
arrogant and innocent (we were twenty-
three; twenty-seven).

Every time a hangover killed more brain cells
I'd come by when it was decently teatime;
he'd put on the kettle and we'd indulge in
the Higher Gossip.

Yes, who slept with whom—but the evolution
of their consciousness, intuition, taste in
china ? (Please, Bill!) interested us more than
heartbreak and cruising.

He was from Virginia: Spode was a factor.
I came from chipped earthenware in the Bronx, but
we were kindred outcasts (Genet); Stendhal and
Proust realigned us.

Hippies in the Haight, faggots in Japantown—
ignorant colonialists: the '60s—
lesbians (before the Mission) in Oakland.
I hadn't met them.

Oh, I knew, but couldn't know, docks, parks, "tearooms,"
parallel to crushes, marriages, passions,
where my sister-spirits, my sometime-lovers
lived out their dream-lives.

My life, in comparison, was one-sided.
Soon I met the lesbians out in Oakland.
(Bill—"La donn' e' mobile"—hummed the Verdi
aria, tone-deaf.)

Decades: you ask, AIDS? Bill, one year, went bankrupt
buying twelve-place services, Spode and Wedgwood,
in a three-roomed flat, no room for them, half his
friends dead or dying.

It takes less than death to inter a friendship
though it feels like death: the unfinished paintings
stacked in mini-storage, the china sold and
our correspondence

buried in a library file. "La donn' e'
mobile." I brew Lapsang Souchong, fragrant
as a smoky memory, while a kitchen
resonates music.

A Farewell to the Finland Woman

i.m. Karig Sára 1917–1999

sad is Eros, builder of cities
and weeping anarchic Aphrodite.
—W. H. Auden, "In Memory of Sigmund Freud"

Two thousand orphans, real ones and children of
Jewish deported parents, so you and your
    ill-sorted Red Cross wartime colleagues
    made it your business to feed and save them.

Blackout: You hacked up dray horses killed in the
air raids, and brought the meat to the orphanage:
    black market lamb a butcher comrade
    donated, you told suspicious children.

Interned in '53 as a Trotskyist
you underwent a double mastectomy
    for "lumpy breasts": chloroform was the
    one anesthetic used in the gulag.

Pain wasn't something you ever dwelled upon.
Most probably, your breasts weren't cancerous—
    Tubercular and convalescent
    you were excused from the mines and road work.

So you were put to work in the bindery.
You'd bound a Russian engineer's personal
    notebook in a silk scarf you'd hidden:
    proving your competence (proof you loved her)

and every evening, you warned the prisoners
who was in danger: punishment, overwork.
    You'd sworn, of course, you read no Russian
    —just a Hungarian female convict.

When I knew you, you liked your flat chest: you had
two inside pockets sewn in each suit jacket.
　　You and the engineer exchanged long
　　letters: your model for prose was Chekhov.

Your six-room Buda-side-of-the-Danube flat
reminded me of rooms in the Bronx which were
　　East Europe reinvented, purplish
　　overstuffed furniture, steamy laundry

hung in the bathroom on a contraption with
pulleys. You drank me under the table each
　　night; I could hear you, every morning
　　back at the typewriter at six-thirty.

What were you writing, decades of mornings when
you were a senior editor, polyglot
　　translator, advocate for writers,
　　war hero, fabulist, solitary—

plays, novels, poems, autobiography?
Your published work: translations and book reviews—
　　who'll tell what you would not have called your
　　adventures, now that the typing's over?

You fell in love with Catherine the communist
Countess in Budapest, and you followed her
　　back to the South of France. You called her
　　Angel, she used your first name; gave orders.

Words were the way she let you make love to her.
She was a wicked octogenarian
　　who'd flirt with anything that moved, but
　　you were her Parsifal, chaste and loyal.

I met you there, one summer I worked at a
card table on a terrace that overlooked
    wild grapevines, fig trees, scrub oak, sheltered
    fluvial passage and small beasts' roving

—light-years away from air raids, Siberia
and antebellum Marxist utopias
    you and your young friends once constructed
    late, in cafés, in your first, true language.

We spoke in English. (French you disdained for an
unavowed reason: Vichy? The armistice?)
    She sometimes spoke to you in Russian,
    sometimes Hungarian, deep-voiced, urgent.

She took an overdose of barbiturates
the morning you were leaving for Switzerland
    together: she was ninety-two. You
    mourned her, and put her affairs in order.

It was her daughter, eighty herself this year,
who told me that, this April, in Budapest
    you died, in the banal suburban
    site of your family-bound last exile.

One day, in '83 when I visited,
a dark-eyed, buxom, curly-haired novelist
    came with her newest book to give you,
    sat like a niece on the purple sofa.

She'd been a two-year-old in the orphanage:
her parents, Jewish deportees, left her there.
    You read her name forty years later
    on a much better list: writers' prizes.

But it was she remembered and searched for you,
insisted that you hear her encomiums.
    Partisan, scribe and second mother:
    motherless, childless, you made each other

possible. Without you, less is possible.
You'd disagree. Your monuments, elegies:
    heroes invent themselves from daily
    womanhood, though they lose breasts and borders.

Ghazal on Half a Line by Adrienne Rich

In a familiar town, she waits for certain letters,
working out the confusion and the hurt in letters.

Whatever you didn't get—the job, the girl—
rejections are inevitably curt in letters.

This is a country with a post office
where one can still make oneself heard in letters.

(Her one-street-over neighbor's Mme de Sévigné
who almost always had the last word in letters.)

Was the disaster pendant from a tongue
one she might have been able to avert in letters?

Still, acrimony, envy, lust, disdain
are land mines the unconscious can insert in letters.

Sometimes more rage clings to a page than she would claim—
it's necessary to remain alert in letters

(an estranged friend donated to a library
three decades of her dishing out the dirt in letters)

and words which resonate and turn within
the mind can lie there flattened and inert in letters.

The tightest-laced precisely-spoken celibate
may inadvertently shrug off her shirt in letters.

Ex-lovers who won't lie down naked again
still permit themselves to flirt in letters.

What does Anonymous compose, unsigned
at night, after she draws the curtain? Letters.

Omelette

> You can't break eggs without making an omelette
> —*That's what they tell the eggs.*
> —RANDALL JARRELL, "A War"

First, chop an onion and sauté it separately
in melted butter, unsalted, preferably.
    Add mushrooms (add girolles in autumn)
    Stir until golden and gently wilted.

Then, break the eggs as neatly as possible,
crack! on the copper lip of the mixing bowl;
    beat, frothing yolks and whites together,
    thread with a filet of cream. You've melted

more butter in a scrupulous seven-inch
iron skillet: pour the mixture in swiftly, keep
    flame high as edges puff and whiten.
    Lower the flame to a reminiscence.

When I was twenty, living near Avenue
D, there were Sunday brunches at four o'clock.
    Eggs were the necessary protein
    hangovers (bourbon and pot) demanded.

Style: that's what faggots (that's what they called themselves)
used to make dreary illness and poverty
    glitter. Not scrambled eggs, not fried eggs:
    Jamesian omelettes, skill and gesture.

Soon after, "illness" wouldn't mean hangovers.
How many of those glamorous headachy
    chefs sliding perfect crescents onto
    disparate platters are middle-aged now?

Up, flame, and push the edges in carefully:
egg, liquid, flows out toward the perimeter.
    Now, when the center bubbles thickly
    spoon in the mushroom and onion mixture—

though the Platonic ideal omelette
has only hot, loose egg at its heart, with fresh
    herbs, like the one that Lambert Strether
    lunched on, and fell for that lost French lady.

Those were the lunchtime omelettes Claire and I
(three decades after the alphabet avenue
    brunch) savored at the women's bookshop/
    salon de thé, our manila folders

waiting for coffee—Emily Dickinson's
rare tenses and amphibious metaphors.
    Browned, molten gold ran on the platter:
    a homely lyric, with salad garland.

Outside, it rained in June, or was spring for a
brief February thaw. Now the bookshop's one
    more Left Bank restaurant, with books for
    "atmosphere": omelettes aren't served there. . . .

With (you've been using it all along) a wood
spatula, flip one half of the omelette
    over the girolle-garnished other.
    Eat it with somebody you'll remember.

Maggy Calhoun

Black/olive argyle cotton, long-sleeved, cropped
at the waist, a bleach-blot in the weave
where some morning's urgent coffee slopped
over what I was reading onto its sleeve.
I'd put it on over my old black jeans
wet, gray July mornings at the gîte
in Mailly-le-Château, discreetly head
for the counter of the one café-
tabac, before submitting to a day
overdetermined by Americans.
The caffeine jolt was perfumed by Gitanes
smoked by the patron while counting out
the just-delivered *Yonne Républicaine*,
and, from the bakery next door, by bread.

French Food

para Rafael

Mostly it starts as peasant food like your
fried plantains, ropa vieja, asapao—
"There's no part of a pig that can't be used,"
more often farmyard porker than wild boar,
but both have got ears, trotters, kidneys, guts.
You'd let your tough old hen or sinewy
beef diced with onion, garlic, lard, potato,
simmer in rough red plonk that's everyday
fare for farmers, part of a soldier's rations—
why vineyards first were planted by the Romans.
Turnips, onions, parsnips, cabbage, beets;
down south, tomatoes, aubergines, courgettes:
what grows reliably, proliferates
(attracting rabbits, those edible vermin).
Your capon might roast in the baker's oven
till you all came back from the fields at noon.
Now another system is imposed:
CEOs of MacDo and Pizza Hut
affirm on the financial page: "Your children
will eat this, whether you like it or not."

Alto Solo

Dear one, it's a while since you turned the lights out
on the porch: a decade of separate summers
passed and cast shed leaves on whatever river
carried our letters.

Merely out of habit, I sometimes tell you
when I've learned a word, made a friend, discovered
some small park where old men debate the headlines,
heard some good music

—it's like jazz, which, even at its most abstract
has the blues in it, has that long saudade
like a memory of what didn't happen
someplace that might be

inlaid with mosaics of recollection
which, in fact's a street corner of the utmost
ordinariness, though the late light steeps it
in such nostalgia

I can hear a saxophone in the background
wail an elegy for the revolution
as someone diminishes in the distance
and the film's over.

Now you know there won't be another love scene.
Do those shadows presage undreamt-of war years?
Twenty, thirty pass, and there's still a sound track
behind the credits:

Cecil Taylor's complex riffs on the keyboard
which a prep-school blonde, seventeen, named Julie
sneaked me into the Blue Note for, because she
knew how to listen—

or it could be Janis packing the Fillmore
West with heartbreak, when I knew that I'd see her
playing pool again at Gino and Carlo's
some weekday midnight.

This is not about you at all: you could be
anybody who died too young, who went to
live in São Paolo or back to Warsaw
or just stopped calling.

(Why did Alice Coltrane stop cutting records?
—think of Pharaoh Sanders being your sideman!—
Lapidary grief: was its consolation
all stone, all silence?)

Now it's morning, gray, and at last a storm came
after midnight, breaking the week-long dog days.
Though I woke at three with a splitting headache,
I lay and listened

to the rain, forgave myself some omissions
as the rain forgave and erased some squalor
It was still too early for trucks and hoses.
A thud of papers

dropped outside the news agent's metal shutters.
Am I glad we didn't last out the winter?
You, the street I made believe that I lived on
have a new address.

Who I miss: the girl of a long-gone season
like my sturdy six-year-old in her OshKosh
overalls, attaining the age of reason
and senior Lego.

You've become—and I never would have wished it—
something like a metaphor of the passage
(time, a cobbled alley between two streets which
diverge, a tune that

reemerges out of the permutations
rung on it by saxophone, bass and piano,
then takes one more plunge so its resolution's
all transformation).

Someone's always walking away; the music
changes key, the moving men pack the boxes.
There the river goes with its bundled cargo:
unanswered letters.

Vendanges

for Geneviève Pastre

The spiral of a story in an ear:
September, two years after the armistice
that ended the disastrous drôle de guerre.
A veteran, convinced to reenlist,
(he'd have a good pension when he retired)
your father, fifty, was a prisoner.
Morning: in the small vineyard that was his,
three sisters and their mother, out with shears
and a basket, cutting table grapes
on the slope below the Causse. This year
(you are the middle sister, seventeen)
you'd be going into hypokhâgne
at the Lycée Fénélon. A line
of men came up the hill, intent as ants,
in stained and dusty Wehrmacht uniforms.
They trudged up toward the Pas de L'Escalette.
You pictured that strait rocky pass, a site
for maquisards in ambush? When you turned,
you saw Françoise's face was white as paste.
Standing before your mother, gaunt, sunburned
and muddy, was a German officer.
He wiped his palms, schoolboyish, on his pants
and, in approximate, respectful French
requested, not demanded, food from her
(if his request could not be a command).
She cut a bunch of grapes with the knife-blade
shears, both lustrous in the morning shade.
He took it, thanked her, backed off, and diminished
to be reintegrated in the line as

it snaked up toward the Causse. Her trembling hand
clutching the sécateurs, dropped to her skirt.
Half-moons under her armpits, and a stench
of fear on the breeze. She held her shoulders braced.
"I thought of your father," she half-explained
and half-implored, looking down at the dirt.

At school, they had you tear out all of Heine's
poems from the text of German poetry.
He was a decadent; he was a Jew.
The teachers could not teach his work—but you
could read the excised pages on your own.
At least you thought that was what they implied,
and read the poems, and memorized a few
and wrote an (unread) essay when you'd finished.

In forty-five, your father, fifty-five
came home. Most of the other prisoners died.
Frost-bitten, kidneys shot, he was alive.
You were an agrégée, rebellious, grown;
barely interrogated his silence.
When he learned about the deportees,
betrayed, stripped of their rank as citizens
as if humanity could be revoked,
his story went into the family's
armoire with patched sheets, has not been aired since.
Years later, you became the one who spoke.

You are a writer in your seventies.
The spiral of a story in your ear
for once is not a story of your own.
A friend, a translator of Japanese,
showed you a just-published inédit
by a late Nippon master, who was

your sister's lover: that same dark-browed Françoise
who died of breast cancer at forty-three
after a decade in Kyoto. He
claimed she had been an "incident," naïve
enough to wait for him, enough to grieve
when he married. She made his language hers.
And his story?
                    A German officer,
half-starved, enters a garden, where a French
farm woman, all alone and almost young,
is picking fruit. In his few words of her tongue
he asks for sustenance. She cuts a bunch
of grapes for him. He remembers her
for years. He goes back after the war
(unharmed, presumably denazified)
to find her. She, of course, has disappeared.

You imagine the scene that this inferred:
the way she would have told it, with an ocean
between her and her sisters and her mother
in a noncognate language she had mastered:
fear breaching the brief maternal garden,
the writer's mind already moving past her,
filing her story, their intimacy
erased in the retelling, as the three
sisters are gone. An emblematic woman
(but with the largesse of her devotion
for the now doubly absent prisoner,
and her fear, too, now given to the invader)
remains, the icon that, somehow, he made her
into, even if he made it for her.

You don't have to imagine how she died.
You were with her. Your grief is mandatory
and quotidian. But you would rather
uncoil a spiral of the path that brought her
back to the Causse. Dawn rain left the hillside
scented with pine and sage. Wind in a hurry
to move whispered the headlines in patois:
transhumance, harvest, an absence of war
as if it were itself an absent father.
A woman in an orchard with three daughters
imagining a man somewhere who suffered,
the dust-bloomed grapes that nonetheless she proffered
to an intrusive and familiar other:
What can you do but tell someone the story?

ITINERANTS

Square du Temple

Artery of the workaday Marais,
the rue de Bretagne leads past the Square
du Temple. The sun burned off the clouds, the air
is brisk and chilly for the end of May.
Released, like springs, school's out, the children play
on grass, in sand, on pavement, everywhere
dashing and dodging, charging the atmosphere
with light; like ancients, bidding the light to stay.
"My own breath"—in this book—"impelled me 'write!'"
A car backfires: massed pigeons take flight
perch on the green-tiled dome of the bandshell,
soar back, V-flocked, to the arboreal
perimeter's stained boughs and re-alight.
The book unwrites itself, whiter than night. . . .

Quai de Valmy

The 3ème becomes the 10ème and 11ème
on the other side of the Place de la République:
beyond that, the canal St. Martin, color of piss and phlegm,
is slow and local. The tow bridges squeak
back against the lock walls and let a low barge wallow
in and wait as the water floods down from the lock
until it's level with the one that follows;
the stout lock keeper trudges importantly back a block
to his bridge, and the barge slides one square tub closer to
the tunnel under the Boulevard Jules Ferry.
I lean on the railing and wait for it to disappear
since I don't think I have anything pressing to do
as the clouds suddenly break and the sky comes clear
with a January afternoon's brief clarity.

On the Stairway

My fourth-floor neighbor, Mme Uyttebroeck-
Achard, a widow in her seventies,
wears champagne-froth lace sheaths above her knees
and patent-leather boots, and henna-red-
orange curls down to the white laminated
collar of her raincoat, like a striptease
artiste who's forgotten whom she needs to please.
She looks a lot like Violette Leduc.
On the dim stairway where she's paused and set
her shopping bags down, the aide-ménagère
for Mme Magin-Levacher, upstairs
one more flight, says Mme Uyttebroeck-Achard's "pas nette"—
not meaning "clean," but, in her dealings, "clear"
—and I think of that muddy genius, Violette.

Promeneurs

hommage aux deux Jacques R.

As I sat on the Quai de Jemmapes
looking back at the Quai de Valmy
with quadrilled cahier on my knee
I could see a gray man in a cap
with a similar book on his lap
on the other side, opposite me.
I'd been writing in mine—so had he.
When I shut my notebook and got up
(having screwed the black top on my Bic)
he walked off at a comfortable clip,
or he would have. But I was unique
and the bench on the opposite quai
remained empty. A crow flew away
over the Hôpital St Louis.

Rue des Écouffes

The street is narrow, and it just extends
rue de Rivoli/rue des Rosiers
a street from which the children went away
clutching their mothers, looking for their friends—
on city buses used for other ends
one not-yet-humid morning in July.
Now kosher butchers coexist with gay
boutiques, not gaily. Smooth-cheeked ephebes hold hands.
Small boys with forelocks trail after bearded men—
and I have dragged that story in again
and will inevitably next compare
the curtains of the creaky balcony
smelling of female exile, exhaled prayer
with the discreet shutters of the women's bar.

Les Scandaleuses

for M.G.H.

Hung on the exposed brown stone of the bar's
back wall, words and collage on aquarelle
metaphor a landscape or a well-
traveled sky, thigh, eye with a view of stars:
her latest work. A child between two wars,
she learned her own vision from the salty squall
of Norman winters, learned what she couldn't tell
except with brush, chalk, pencil, engraver's
stylus and blade, with ink spilled on a stone
as the sea spills up and over the stones when the tide
comes in. Leather jacket, cap, she stands, briefly alone
at the bar with a glass of wine, her Celtic moon-
stone eyes as light and dark as the shapes she made
while the night's first women come in out of the rain.

Les Scandaleuses II

The night's first women come in out of the rain:
two couples who arrived, enlaced, astride
two motorcycles, pulled up just outside
the door, doff helmets and leather, order gin/
tonic, beer, beer, a kir. From the bar, they crane
their necks toward the row of dreams, mindscapes, implied
back roads they're too young to have traveled; slide
closer together, wanting things to begin.
Watching, she doesn't envy them their youth,
their way of being in a pack, in pairs
(wounds inflicted, in the name of "truth,"
on friends, near-infidelities on stairs).
But the lacework beginning near that one's mouth
is elegant. Engraver's grooves. Soft dares.

Nulle part

The elegant engraver's grooves: soft dares
to follow down to the glass-roofed quai, embark
on the last train's last car hurtling through the dark
tunnel irregularly blazed with flares
alizarin, viridian. Lit by the glare's
a silhouette, androgynous, at work
setting (in Paris? London? Prague? New York?)
mosaic tiles. She leads you up spiral stairs
into the blue explosion of the air's
matinal brilliance. But she disappears—
avid flesh, mercurial avatar
desire or imagination sends?
And then you know exactly where you are:
the street is narrow; you see where it ends.

Square du Temple II

Moon on late daylight: green fruit plucked from a stalk.
Almost July; almost the end of cherry
season. I walked out on a literary
cocktail early, because I couldn't make more small talk
and because it's a pervasive joy to walk
across the square at not-yet-dusk. Its tutelary
geniuses, preadolescent, very
slender and supple African children, hawk-
swoop on skates around the resting lawn.
(The toddlers and their guardians have gone
home.) A breeze flies from their shoulder blades,
loquacious and invisible, in banners.
The duck pond is refreshed by small cascades,
as silence cures an overdose of manners.

Rue Beaurepaire

On a wide side street that leads to the canal
job-seeking Meridional families,
retired mail clerks, philoprogenitive Chinese
textile workers, Tunisian grocers
have found an issue everyone agrees
to disagree on—IV drug users'
right to a safe haven among neighbors:
a hostel instead of a hospital
ER, with coffee, washing machines and showers,
a Moroccan intern who serves as nurse,
weekly rap groups, small tables to converse
across. From balconies, spanning the street,
hang homemade banners, spray paint on white sheets:
send them to another street—not ours.

Rêve champêtre

If, in the Cité Dupetit-Thouars
there were a three-roomed flat for sale, I would
leave my tourist-infested neighborhood
for semi-rural quiet off the Square
du Temple. You can only drive a car
in if you live there. Next to a dusty wood-
worker's shop's an ancient saddlery.
Behind a shop front, two gray women were
turning clay on wheels that softly whined.
Stiff blue hydrangeas stood importantly
on guard on windowsills; on a clothesline
two work shirts flapped above a cobbled yard.
(It's not five minutes from the Cyber Bar,
and, in the rue du Temple, Monoprix.)

Rue Beaurepaire II

The banners across the rue Beaurepaire
are gone, those "for" and also those "against"
the shop-front drop-in center. Someone's rinsed
away the angry slogans spray-painted
across the elegant discreet façade
stenciled with quotations from Voltaire,
Sartre, Aragon, Camus. The mayor
stayed out of it: nobody was convinced
and rumor once more outweighed evidence.
(The school's one street over—really, next door!
Don't they have AIDS? Dealers will come. They'll steal . . .)
They won't be driven into the canal;
just relocated to the Gare du Nord
a site indicative of transience—

—according to the ACT UP bulletin.
But on a brilliant summer afternoon
below the white, newly anonymous
façade, the door was open nonetheless.
In the doorway, two women and a man
were talking. One woman, I guessed,
might be a client, so I went on past
and sat by the canal, which, in the sun,
looked less like bodily effluvium;
a few discreet minutes later, returned.
The young man, dressed in orange, fresh on brown/
olive skin, was the intern who'd been there last June.
They're backed now by la Ligue des Droits de l'Homme;
keep clinic hours, but quietly. They've learned.

Rue de Bretagne

after Jacques Roubaud

That afternoon in the rue de Bretagne
(I think back often to that afternoon)
I pushed a shopping cart through Monoprix
where anything you'd like to eat or own—
Roquefort or bath FA, shrink-wrapped lots of three
bottles of Badoit, pâté de campagne,
a coffeemaker engineered by Braun,
is there to contemplate, covet and buy.
Fulfillment in a supermarket's fast:
would that it were desire's paradigm,
I thought, in line, sure that a stretch of time
could, like the summer's evening sunlight, last
on an uncomplicated day in June
remembering those lines of Aragon.

26 rue de Turenne/ 26 December

Across the street, the widow weighs the storm
that woke her in predawn dark when the wind
rattled her tall old windows. Lights blink on
in other buildings: flares. A car alarm
enters the howling, full of screech and thud:
clay on macadam, glass on metal, wood
on plastic. A café awning rips, flaps.
A green trash can skids down the street. She wraps
a moth-eaten blue shawl that she peels from
an armchair around her, covering her head.
It seems as if she's always lived alone.
It's ten years, or two months, that he's been dead.
Her grandmother's chandelier tinkles behind
her, seasick, swaying like a pendulum.

Turenne/ Francs-Bourgeois

A winter Tuesday morning: people shopped
with damp dogs bundling under their purchases
in light rain, fine as an unspoken wish
while merchants scoured and scrubbed their premises.
From behind the jazz-club's curtained door
held open with a bucket and a mop,
a Yorkshire terrier surged out and frisked
and yipped around the tweedy-elegant
heels of a couple with a Lab, that risked
a curious butt-sniff, also punishment.
The thin-lipped woman whipped the Labrador
across the nose, but only with the leash.
The dog whimpered and cringed. A passer-by
across the street from them began to cry.

Troisième sans ascenseur

A square of sunlight on the study wall
is worth her notice, so she makes a note.
Various printings of the books she wrote
fill shelves encroaching on the narrow hall
but not her work-room: that's spare, practical.
Six dictionaries, *Bartlett's Familiar Quot-*
ations, typewriter. Seventy-eight,
she's a technician of grammatical
rules in three languages, and that will do.
The desk is a librarian's, blonde oak.
The angle of her chair, turned toward a stack
of fine-lined blank notebooks, leads her eyes to
the bare wall blazing with its pristine one
tall north window, framing the winter sun.

Librairie L'Arbre à lettres

The February noon was more like March.
A wind that smelled marine pushed a soak-through
rain in from nowhere, veiling a gaze as blue
as hydrangeas around a fieldstone church
which I was content to notice more than watch
while browsing in Biography and New
Releases in the bookshop on the bou-
levard du Temple: an aleatoric search
for a novel cited in *Le Monde.*
Books are clannish; I wasn't *sans famille*
opening that one. The rain thinned; the rain stopped.
An afternoon proposed itself to me.
My serviceable brown umbrella dripped
dry, as the sky cleared, in the umbrella stand.

Troisième sans ascenseur ailleurs

The cold rain falls and fell all afternoon
the way it fell through the last months of winter.
In twos and threes, my friends are out of town
for Easter weekend. Tourists take the center
over, gloved and scarved—speaking Italian
and Portuguese: they've holidays as well.
How stubbornly the fuchsia rhododendron
in the square blooms in unseasonable
cold, how stubbornly the squadron
of swallows swoops between volleys of rainfall.
But I'm imagining their flight—I think
them flying, from a hard-backed chair behind
pine table, windows, Bach, books, gone to ground.
The late gray sky darkens. I want a drink.

Square du Temple: Another August

Two long-legged black girls jump double-Dutch
in turn on a stretch-band looped over the fence
around the lawn. A high-cheekboned intense
and Slavic-looking pregnant woman touch-
es the white bandanna on her hair, her much-
dog-eared Pascal closed on her lap. Her pants'
black satin sets off the magnificence
of her high-tech running shoes. We watch
three Chinese toddler boys circle and circle
the bandshell, holding hands, singing *Marlbrough
s'en va-t'en guerre*. A stout young African-
print clad brown mother kicks a soccer ball
to her small boy and girl who kick it back.
When will the moment be enough again?

Place des Vosges: October

There is memory, and there's the haze
of misted afternoon becoming memory
if you're lucky, on a damp October day
you wish were just one of a string of October days
in the same city, at the same address:
small spark no one is likely to take away
of appetite for a conversation, curiosity
about the nights and thoughts that bronzed a face.
In the square, beneath unleafing horse-chestnut trees
autumnal as yourselves, but acquiescent,
you trash a notable lapsed Communist.
Your friend says, "Turncoats sell their ass to the flies
and then complain that history is unjust."
For a breath of paradox, you are in the present.

DESESPERANTO

Grief

Grief walks miles beside the polluted river,
grief counts days sucked into the winter solstice,
grief receives exuberant schoolyard voices
as flung despisals.

It will always be the first of September.
There will be Dominican boys whose soccer
game provides an innocent conversation
for the two people

drinking coffee, coatless. There will be sunset
roselight on the river like a cathedral.
There will be a rusty, amusing tugboat
pushing a barge home.

Did she think she knew what her friend intended?
Did she think her brother rejoiced to see her?
Did she think she'd sleep one more time till sunrise
holding her lover?

Grief has got no brother, sister or lover.
Grief finds friendship elsewhere. Grief, in the darkened
hours and hours before light flicks in one window
holds grief, a mirror.

Brother? He was dead, in a war-drained city.
Grief was shelling peas, with cold water running
in the sink; a harpsichord trilled Corelli
until the phone rang.

And when grief came home from a post-op nightwatch
two small girls looked reticent over homework.

Half the closet, half the drawers were empty.
Who was gone this time?

Grief is isolationist, short-viewed. Grief lacks
empathy, compassion, imagination;
reads accounts of massacres, floods and earthquakes
mired in one story.

Grief is individual, bourgeois, common
and banal, two women's exchange in Sunday
market: "Le mari de Germaine est mort." They
fill bags with apples.

Grief is primagravida, in her fifth month.
Now she knows the fetus has died inside her.
Now she crosses shopping-streets on a sun-shot
mid-winter morning.

Winter licks the marrow from streets that open
onto parks and boulevards, rivers, river-
parallel parkways, arteries to bridges,
interstates, airports.

Grief daubs kohl on middle-aged burning eyelids.
Grief drives miles not noticing if the highway
runs beside an ocean, abandoned buildings
or blackened wheatfields

—and, in fact, she's indoors. Although her height is
average, massive furniture blocks and crowds her:
oak and pine, warm gold in their grain she thought would
ransom her season.

Workmen clear a path to repair the windows,
not with panes of light on their backs, no message-

bearers these. Still stubbornly green, a street leads
back to the river.

Fourteen years drained into the fifteen minutes
that it took a late summer sun to douse its
light behind the opposite bank, the boys to
call their match over.

Chanson de la mal aimée

December fog condensed above the Seine.
Though it was not the season to atone
for sins, for my sins (unknown) the tears began
again. Unknown, as another mind's unknown
till written, shouted, sung, spray-painted: spoken.
Perhaps (why we all cry) unknown even then.
I walked toward my own bed that I slept and woke in
across that river, or another one.

Between harp-cables humming toward Brooklyn
we were, we thought, descendants of Hart Crane,
emancipated, nocturnal, nineteen.
The city's nightwatch glistened on either side.
Streetlights were haloed by the damp and dawn.
Shadows beneath implied what they implied.
Once we arrived, we'd just turn back again
across that river, or another one.

I crossed the Thames in taxis for a man
who lived quite well without me in South London.
Later there was a girl who heard a train
head north, beneath red leaves, along the Hudson.
The Joyce Bridge on the Liffey one damp June
morning stretched forward like a conversation
I'd no reason to think would not go on
across that river, or another one.

A fresh breeze from the arm of the Malvan
fingered across the terrace of the stone
house where a card table sat in the sun
at which I wrote, bare-chested, dripping sweat.

A Gauloise smouldered out in the Cinzan-
o ashtray. Soft hiss, like the cigarette:
a bird rushed up through oak leaves and was gone
across that river or another one.

The Seine descends from sources in the Yonne;
The children of Vincelles and Vincelottes
launched lanterns cradling candles, let them float
downriver, to begin the village fête.
There would be fireworks, in the misty rain.
A couple on the terrace of the inn
mourned someone as the fireflies blinked out
across that river, or another one.

The Hudson saw my heart break. The Hudson
took it, discarded garbage on its swells.
I'm leaving you. There is nobody else.
She lied she lied she lied she lied she lied.
Walk away from the river, shaking, stunned
as you once came back to it, glad bride,
found child, proud friend. Sewage seeped and spread
across that river, or another one.

There is no heaven and it has no Queen
(There is no God and Mary is His Mother).
I have one life and one is all I get;
it will be "same" unless I make it "other."
The workings of the wind, so intricate,
augmented to a night of devastation.
Water bloated the banks, with bridges down
across that river or another one.

Betrayal isn't torture, cancer, rape.
Authorities don't gas abandoned wives;

deplore the ones who put their heads in stoves
(still, don't suggest it to the Taliban).
Betrayal is a dull stereotype.
"The friends who met here and embraced are gone /
each to his own mistake . . ." (that's wartime Auden)
across that river or another one

I crossed the Pont Sully, above the Seine,
below a small, bright, distant winter moon
tasting the conversation and the room,
glad that my lungs were clear again, and wine
had flavor, that I wanted to walk home
at midnight, that walking home alone
at midnight was a privilege of mine
across that river or another one.

Explication de texte

Plusieurs réponses sont possibles, mais montrez comment
la ville peut se lire comme un substitut de l'objet désiré.
—Text on Apollinaire for lycéens preparing the baccalauréat

Paris nights, drunk on gin,
aflame with electrical fire.
Trolleys with green-lit spines
sing their long route down wire
and rail, deranged machines.
—GUILLAUME APOLLINAIRE; trans. M.H.

Paris is wintery gray.
The small rain spits and sputters.
Before the break of day
when green trucks hose the gutters
lights go on in the bakery.

The days go on, routine
light lingers on the clocks
Yellow and red and green
crowd in the window box
impermanent and benign.

The tiny sans-abri
and her more substantial friend
arrive from a night on the quay
at their avenue, extend
their hands to earn their pay,

each on her opposite side.
They've been on the street together
for over a decade
while others jettisoned other
partners and promises made.

Bickering all the way
but punctual at their labors
weekday and holiday
they are my long-term neighbors
with Mme de Sévigné

The days go on, routine.
I would be happy never
to board another plane.
My feet, crossing the river,
and the La Défense/Vincennes

line, or Balard-Creteil
are forms of transportation
quite adequate for me.
Other communication
failed: well, let it be.

Sorrow becomes a sink
and loss becomes a drain.
The drain begins to stink.
Call the plumber again.
Remember how to think.

The poet who wrote and longed
for a woman he barely knew
by whom he thought he'd been wronged
gave Paris new verses to
her electrical torch-song:

the weedy, lovelorn merman's
complaint to pitiless sirens,
some similes, some sermons,
Montmartre and environs
—he even included Germans.

(I know the Rhône a bit;
I do not know the Rhine.
Proximity to it
gave ancestors of mine
the thought of a way out.)

When friends say what they mean
companionship illumines
nights that unroll, routine
in being scaled for humans
choosing their food and wine.

We ordered a house pichet
and argued down to the wire at
a smoke-stained brown café:
my friend looked more like the pirate
than the pirate's fiancée.

Poached salmon followed soup
while another loquacious friend
talked such amazing shop
we left the "Vagenende"
when the waiters were cleaning up.

Days and nights, routine
as unambiguous words:
accompanied, alone,
the hours are not like swords,
strike gently, like the rain.

I have two pairs of glasses:
for the peopled world beyond
the panes; for the small world this is
where I eat, and read *Le Monde*,
and drink, and the evening passes.

I grill my trout. I drink
three glasses of Brouilly
or some adequate Southwest plonk.
A Mozart symphony
drowns out the screech and honk

of buses, bikes and vans
and the selfsame garbage truck,
manned by green-clad Africans
come back at nine o'clock
to empty the big green cans.

Paris, elegant gray
godmother, consolation,
heartbroken lullaby,
smell of the métro station,
you won't abandon me.

A hot bath; Couperin:
the hours are not like swords,
strike gently, like the rain,
notes on a harpsichord,
impermanent, benign.

Migraine Sonnets

entre chien et loup

It's a long way from the bedroom to the kitchen
when all the thought in back of thought is loss.
How wide the dark rooms are you walk across
with a glass of water and a migraine
tablet. Sweat of hard dreams: unforgiven
silences, missed opportunities.
The night progresses like chronic disease,
symptom by symptom, sentences without pardon.
It's only half past two, you realize.
Five windows are still lit across the street.
You wonder: did you tell as many lies
as it now appears were told to you?
And if you told them, how did you not know
they were lies? Did you know, and then forget?

There were lies. Did you know, and then forget
if there was a lie in the peach orchard? There was the lie
a saxophone riffed on a storm thick summer sky,
there was the lie on a postcard, there was the lie thought
and suggested, there was the lie stretched taut
across the Atlantic, there was the lie that lay
slack in the blue lap of a September day,
there was the lie in bed, there was the lie that caught
its breath when it came, there was the lie that wept.
There was the lie that read the newspaper.
There was the lie that fell asleep, its clear
face relaxing back to the face of a child.
There was the lie you held while you both slept.
A lie hung framed in the doorway, growing wild.

The face framed in the doorframe is a wild
card now, mouth could eat silence, mouth could speak
the indigestible. Eyes, oh tourmaline, a crack
in the glass, break the glass. Down a green-tiled
corridor double doors open. Who was wheeled
through, hallucinating on a gurney, weak
with relief as muscle and nerve flickered awake,
while a dreamed face framed in a doorframe opened and
    smiled?
Precisely no one's home. No dog will come
to lay his jowls across bent knees and drool
and smile the black-gummed smile he shares with wolves.
The empty doorframe frames an empty room
whose dim fluorescence is perpetual.
The double doors close back upon themselves.

The double doors close back upon themselves
The watcher from the woods rejoins the pack:
shadows on branches' steely lacework, black
on black, dark ornaments, dark wooden shelves.
Fever-wolves, guardians a lamp dissolves
in pitiless logic, as an insomniac
waits to hear the long night crack and break
into contaminated rusty halves.
This is the ninety-seventh (count) night watch in
the underbrush of hours closed on you since
a lie split open like a rotten fruit.
A metal band around your head begins
to tighten; pain shutters your eyes like too much light.
It's a long way from the bedroom to the kitchen.

Max

Last year I lost a proper name, the name
I answered to, which was my grandfather's
and now am nameless, even in the bad dream

where someone else has all the right answers
and I am wrong and wrong and nothing that's
true was true and every last word's hers:

bad dreams like costive shit from sluggish guts,
the residue of loss. More things I lost:
savoy sausages with hazelnuts;

a brindled pit bull bounding for a tossed
ball in the dog run; Korean groceries'
lilacs in buckets under car exhaust

on Broadway, a blossoming line of cherry trees,
a key in a lock, a twilight saxophone
positing lyrical philosophies

of meditation, of revolution;
the right of way on a square mile of streets
someone might do their shopping on with someone;

desire not dried and shriveled by regrets;
the place that I came back to when I came;
the torch singer's trite rhyme of "lust" and "trust";

the beloved child's freedom, that freedom
to spiral farther and farther out from home
since each trajectory loops back toward home

where someone calls her by her proper name.

Road Work

The third week of July
shutters creep closed on the day,
inevitably, slowly.
The citizens go away
to the mountains, to the sea,

to résidences secondaires
or relatives on the farm,
on charters, on guided tours.
(In Belleville, people stay home,
and in the Goutte d'Or

where "charter" is shorthand
for forced expatriation.
Uneasy immigrants
cannot afford vacations
from an unpromised land

which might not take them back
from wars and epidemics.
Their children play in the park
with summer academics'
kids from Berlin and New York.)

Geraniums and fuchsias
stand in the morning sun
Lavender, mauve, their luscious
blooms are dared, then done,
wilt like unuttered wishes.

Once I got off a train
and took the métro to

my stop, Bréguet-Sabin,
and a wave of joy washed through
me, climbing up into the rain

and crossing the rue Amelot.
I said its name out loud
like a good friend's name, although
it's a street where nothing occurred
that touched anyone I know.

Sorrow persists, an itch,
a sore that doesn't heal.
Festering under a patch
of bandage, edges congeal,
could break: try not to scratch.

Mme Levacher upstairs
lives alone with a TV.
Besides her aide-ménagère's
afternoon visits three
times weekly, no one's there

although she has a son
who lives five minutes away
(a robust sixty-one)
above the fromagerie
in the rue Saint-Antoine.

The housekeeper is from
Mauritius. We stop
and talk. I say, I'd come
and visit; I could shop. . . .
We're standing in the dim

light on the spiral stair-
way, which I can still run up
like the young housekeeper.
My room is not a trap.
In its bright book-lined shelter

a dialoguing presence
silenced itself abruptly.
Now absence is the essence
of cycles which unsubtly
suggest the hardest lessons

were not learned very well.
Road work: a jackhammer
tears up the street: the smell
of steaming bacs of tar
invests the café, full

of tourists and a few
neighborhood regulars.
I am both "I" and "thou,"
watching the bulldozers,
I talk about them to

myself, as I've always done,
my own interlocutor.
What's already begun,
a season of departure,
will terminate with mine.

I'll probably come back
less occupied with grief.
Slowly around the block
in a vest like a maple leaf,
with a tall, carved walking stick

comes a cavalier old man
with his wolfish alter ego.
One sits, and one lies down;
one gets water; one, espresso.
One smokes, one sleeps in the sun.

Grief's radical subtraction
enacted, may there be
some countersurge, reaction
of self-sufficient joy
at a rainy intersection.

Paragraph for Hayden

Quadruple bypass: yes, he had it.
What happens next is anybody's guess.
After the surgeon's pre-op visit
he pulled the tubes and needles out, got dressed
and stalked outside to smoke a cigarette.
The surgeon threatened not to operate.
Old heart, old curmudgeon,
old genius, terrified old man
who more than anyone knows form
is one rampart of sanity,
your mind is ringing like a fire alarm
and you still smoke three packs a day.
Not lover, barely friend, from this distance
I break your rule and say,
stay in the present tense. Stay in the present tense.

February 10

Inarticulate, the dream subsides in growls.
Nothing as human as clean sentences.
Nothing as cleansing as repentance. Was
some life left folded into plush blue towels
and 200-plus thread all-cotton sheets
like a housewifely sachet of lavender?
I've learned the answer or I haven't, or
the question balances, repeats, repeats
day after night into the cotton's cool
and solitary folds, the resurrected
light I look into with unprotected
eyes. Sometimes the sky is beautiful.
Sometimes despair is as habitual
as walking in the morning to the train
station to be in class on time, as plain
yogurt, as grapefruit juice, steady and dull
as the seventeenth hour of a migraine
all evening long, still with me when I wake.
And don't I often trigger a headache
refilling glass on solo glass of wine?
Isn't there something clearer about pain
than year-old grief gone tarnished with its dull
blade, with its blotched skin, with its bad smell?
The dusk recedes again, or afternoon
extends itself, life measured against light:
how new, how much repeated, for how long,
whether, and how profoundly, I was wrong,
whether, in what ignorance, I was right.

Ranns

When will some
tutelary image come
spinning in brief silhouette
past the window, blown brown leaf

that's not grief,
vagrant, ragged, cold and stiff?
All the noises of work day
commerce, cars, children's voices

filter up
from the street, crescendo, drop
to an undertone. Now it's
mid-afternoon. Couperin

harpsichord's
song-settings (I know the words):
oh, nameless, impossibly
fair and fickle shepherdess—

who was not
any such thing, but some wit-
ty courtesan, who gossiped
with Mme de Montespan.

My good friend
knows the passages, could find,
as the measures rise and fall,
a balance that she treasures.

Knowing more
of grief than she bargained for;
she'd say again: make black tea,
run a hot bath, read Montaigne.

Almost Equinoctial

The banks of the river are covered in water. It's rained
that much: plane trees up to their waists, the stairs going down
from the quais step onto water, not footpaths. It's rained
through March, daily, on crocus and jonquil, on outthrust
    brown
red-tipped branches, on market-stall awnings. It's rained
on the barges, stopped boat traffic, houseboats are tethered at
    sea.
The path that leads to the Jardin des Plantes down the Quai
Saint-Bernard, past willows and post-cubist bronzes, is
    drowned
for a day, a week. The riverbank amphitheaters are under
mud-colored water, no dog-romps, no kids playing drums
with their Arab or Gallic or Jewish hair twisted in dreads.
The benches are stranded on landspits or islanded. Where
do the pensioners sit, has some café absorbed the clochards?
Will the moon pull the tidewash to sea tonight, will the sun
uncrumple the grass, bake the mud back to footworthy clay?
The Saturday strollers dig their Vibram soles in single file
on the seeping green hummock that clutches the unlikely edge
of the swollen Seine. Holding a cellophane-wrapped bouquet
of orange and white multi-petalled ranunculi
I muddy my good black loafers, too. There's no cause for alarm
yet, no new one, only a usual passage turned strange
in the middle of March on a day when it hasn't rained
yet, that's no longer a relevant anniversary,
on my way to lunch in the south end of the cinquième.

Sonnet on a Line from
Vénus Khoury-Ghata

She recognized the seasons by their texture
like flannel sheets or thick-piled bath-sized towels
like white asparagus or colored vowels
whose scabby bark elicited conjecture.
She recognized the seasons by their light
as flowering plants and bushes, keyed to measure
its length, wake briefly or unroll at leisure
beneath it: even when it's cold, the night
holds off; the long and reminiscent dusk
is like a pardon or a friend returned
whom she thought elsewhere, subtracted forever,
eclipsed in distance. Though the plants can't bask
in heat, darkness delays, and they discern
what equilibrium they can recover.

Quoi de neuf sur la guerre?

(Café Le Diplomate, Turenne/Saint
Claude, March, 2001)

Five old men
dissect last week's election.
Jacques' student granddaughter bought
a studio apartment

—bigger than
the three rooms that he lived in
with his two brothers, parents,
in the rue du Pont-aux-Choux . . .

(two streets up).
Glasses folded on his cap,
Maurice fishes for a not-
quite-lost riposte in Yiddish.

(His accent
is a familiar garment
on a neighbor, here or in
Strauss Park on upper Broadway.)

The senior
four worked here before the war.
Now they're back in the rag trade.
An eleven o'clock break

—tradition:
black coffee and discussion,
the *cheder* relived later.
The one two decades younger,

Victor, will
at last bring up Israel
—sixtyish son asking his
elders what ought to be done.

And Maurice,
the pouches around his eyes
creased deep in a sad smile, says,
having known wars, not much peace,

(a schoolboy
in Krakow in 1930),
"A solution? There is just
one. The final solution."

Does he mean
the British had a plan in
'48: Arabs could finish
Hitler's job in the new state?

Does he mean
genocide in Palestine
to be practiced by "our own"?
Victor changes the subject.

The waitress
interrupts exegesis:
Please pay, her shift is over.
The watchdog of the café,

a boxer,
trails his young boss, stops at her
trim heels. He scowls, sniffs the floor
and gets sawdust on his jowls.

Ghazal

She took what wasn't hers to take: desire
for all that's not her, for what might awake desire.

With it, the day's a quest, a question, answered where-
ever eye, mind lights. Desire seeks, but one can't seek desire.

A frayed wire, a proof, a flame, a drop of globed hot wax,
a riddle solved or not by William Blake: desire.

Erase the film with light, delete the files,
re-reel the story, will all that unmake desire?

For peace or cash, lovers and whores feign lust or climaxes.
A solitary can evoke, but cannot fake desire.

Crave nothing, accept the morning's washed and proffered air
brushing blued eyelids with an oblique desire.

There was an other, an answer, there was a Thou
or there were mutilations suffered for your sake, desire.

Without you, there is no poet, only some nameless hack
lacking a voice without your voice to speak desire.

For the 6th of April

for Marie Ponsot

Eden is
pots and tubs on the terrace.
Tenacious seeds root, wind-strewn,
to bloom around the ficus.

Light and shade
from this and every decade
cross and dapple the notebook
you hold open on your lap.

Eighty? Well,
forty, too, and twenty: still
no one's fool, a canny heart,
spirit joyously at school.

Precocious
child, you run ahead of us
aging enfants terribles of
a later generation

Slim mother
of a brood of boys, you were
(seemed) all honed will, clear mind, like
a boy, hermit, young sybil

while the day-
to-day life of the body
which needs food on the table,
an orderly neighborhood

and wages,
worked through you. You filled pages
nonetheless: fables, lines, rhymes,
hints from all your languages:

how to live
well on bread and wine, forgive
old enemies and lovers
so that full days pass in peace.

Is it luck
no one gets her old life back?
What you regret you redress
if you can; use; don't forget.

Your daughter,
one more city gardener,
tends your best cuttings in pots
in pale sun a half-block west.

Your desk looks
out on your trees (past the books).
Thick thumbs of amaryllis
work their way up and spring comes.

A Sunday After Easter

Ah! que le monde est grand à la clarté des lampes!
Aux yeux du souvenir, que le monde est petit.
—BAUDELAIRE, "Le Voyage"

A child who thought departure would be sweet,
I roam the borders of my neighborhood,
dominical, diminished. Young gay men,
their elbows brushing, Sunday-stroll, in pairs
headed for the weekend flea market
on the boulevard Richard-Lenoir
at Oberkampf. I sit in a café
nursing a decaf. A small Chinese boy
(or girl) in sweats stands on tiptoes to reach
the flippers of the Space Pirates machine.
I want to find some left turn into dream
or story, the next chapter, memory
not saturated with regret, into
a vision as unlikely as the mare
with sweat-soaked roan flanks and a tangled mane,
dragon's breath steaming from her flared nostrils
onto a wind too sharp to call a breeze
cantering riderless across the square
opposite, between the children in
the sandbox and the old men arguing
on benches, in French, in Mandarin,
in Arabic, Yiddish and Portuguese,
despite the afternoon's dour, bone-deep chill,
early February in late April,
except for punctual persistent green

(Fringy and still-fragile auburn fronds
burst from the rhododendron's rubbery
green leaves, red swellings globe the tips
of cherry boughs, japonica blooms
in double yellow stars on bamboo stalks.
The orange crocuses are past their prime
on the lawn, but now the purple ones
emerge, and pansies, with mascaraed petals
in their beds are gold and purple too.
Three early roses, peach-dappled white,
stand out on bushes nearly bare, studded
with sparse, furled, also reddish nascent leaves.)

of trees and shrubs.
                An afternoon when sun
is as unlikely as a riderless
horse to cross the square.
                    Imagine that
it were given back to me to be
the child who knew departure would be sweet,
the boy who drew square-rigged ships, the girl who knew
truck routes from Ottawa to Mexico,
the one who found a door in Latin verse
and made a map out of hexameters.

A young Moroccan or Tunisian
with a thick, kinky auburn pony tail,
vastly pregnant, in an oversized
sweater and cargo pants, a toddler and
an almond-eyed five-year-old in tow,
sits with an older blonde in camel's hair
coat and tailleur, who orders a Sancerre
(the name of the café is "Le Sancerre").

The young mother gets three Oranginas
but the Chinese child and her older son
have found each other (school friends) and begun
to play a giggling round of hide-and-seek.
under the two empty tables between us.
The little one, whose name is Dominique,
slurps Orangina through a straw, and sways
to the loudspeaker's Motown Muzak (O
bars of my girlhood. Ô saisons, ô châteaux),
then slaps his snowpants and begins to howl
"Je veux ma doudoune! Je veux ma cagoule!"
(a child already eager to depart).
"On dit" she tells him gently, "*je voudrais.*"

She reaches in her pants pocket to pay
but the tall blonde has (she's whom to the young mother?).
Bise-bise, the ritual, they leave each other
at the door; the girl, in a long dark-
blue greatcoat crosses the street to the park,
a child tugging each hand; the woman turns
the corner into the rue des Archives,
becomes a shape the falling light discerns.
(One would postulate brown, not nascent leaves,
the color of absinthe, but innocent,
the color of a world renewed, present,
where absence has become a habit and
occasionally less significant
than wind turning a corner, than the frond
from which a bloom breaks, than the old storm-bent
willow skimming the rain-swollen pond.)

The Chinese child is crying silently
but finds the seated couple he or she
belongs to (both are French, white, not-quite-young).
The tear-tracked child and father reinstall
themselves at Space Pirates pinball.
The roan mare pauses, thrusts her head among
the rhododendron bushes, nibbles the tender shoots,
unseen beast nourished on unlikely fruits,
turning her copper head in fits and starts.
And what is riderless in me departs
around the corner, into the next street,
into the afternoon, holding its light
later in each day's cloud-leaded sky.
Or stays, doglike, between the wrought-iron feet
of the small table, ears at the alert,
actively silent, having learned to wait.

Fable

for M.P.

A fox, a badger, any provident creature
clever and agile, knowing how to get through a long
winter and a wet spring, you tapped your foot to the song
Louis Armstrong sang, retrieved on the loudspeaker,
and read the *TLS*, and sipped a strong
mug of French Roast, while outside the café
a fine cold rain inundated upper Broadway
across which your friend ran back and forth, being
vague and distracted and distraught and wrong
about how long precisely it would take
to triage, dismantle, wrap, pack, box and stack
a third of a life in one rain-curtained building:
a wild duck's molting wings flapped in distress
between departure and the *TLS*.

Jean-Michel Galibert,
Épicier à Saint-Jean-de-Fos
for Guy Goffette

Reconstitute a sense to make of absence
in the still heat of noon, south, summer
where spindled years unravel and unwind.
A hound bays behind a fence. An old white van
beached beneath oleander in a yard
rusts where it ran down, where something came to grief.

Some summers, joy illuminated grief
and solitude was savory. Then, absence
was a prelude, then stiff, starched, flag-striped yards
of sheet on a clothesline flapped in a sudden summer
gust, like the curtains on a caravan
parked in the town square, billowing with wind,

while children anticipated drumrolls, wind
instruments, brasses, florid joy and grief
mimed close to home. From the striped awning of a van
whiffs of merguez fried with onions, smell whose absence
would be a small, real rift in the stuff of summer.
Would have been. The dog paces in his three square yards

of territory, the paved part of a yard
where jasmine and oleander wind
their ribboned leaves like schoolgirls starting summer
vacation. Decline "departure," decline "grief,"
compose an essay illustrating absence
using, for instance, the abandoned van

that used to be, let's say, the grocer's van
which parked on Wednesdays opposite the schoolyard
and the children who were present, who were absent.
Women came up in print dresses, cardigans, wind-
breakers, seasons changing, even grief
fading like the painted sign in summer

sun, winter rain. After a few winters, springs, summers
the bright sign was illegible, the van
rusted, someone had grown into grief.
The van is parked in the grocer's son's back yard,
its windows shattered, spiderwebbed. The wind
blows through it, marks itself present in that absence.

The grocer's son sat in the van each summer
morning that first year. Even grief was absent
as the wind unwound the streamers in his yard.

Again, for Hayden

I.

This morning
at five fear seized me and clung
like a leech, a tick, napalm:
what could calm its ravening?

Flicked on the switch
of a round pine bed-lamp which
was wedged among books piled there:
Montaigne, Flaubert, Gallant, Rich

and Carruth.
Either a book or a bath
will do when the hour's a drop
down the slope: loss, age, pain, death.

(A pilot
trapped in the gyring cockpit
or just the old soul upstairs,
ninety years old, losing it.)

I've my own
words, but I read yours: snow, stone,
logs, stars, to push back despair.
I read bear. I read mountain.

I read thaw
when there's rarely enough snow
in this city to warrant
that event—but fear's soft paw

might lift, might
follow the lingering night
off in silence, while named birds
cry their own words and take flight.

II.

I hear the gears of your own old engine,
revving up, growl: this is too damn vague.
Developers blasted your numinous green mountain
in the seventies: highways, log-
jams. And on the rue Saint-Antoine,
M. Latronche, the best traiteur has gone
(retired): no more aubergine
flans, wild-boar ham off the bone.
There's another fast-food, panini-to-go
and Coke, for the tourists.
You walked across your aster-constellated meadow
what may now have been twenty Augusts
ago, counting the losses, noticing
rust, coral, crimson, what changes, what lasts,
what sharpened fear and sorrow into song.

Desesperanto

after Joseph Roth

Parce que c'était lui; parce que c'était moi.
—Montaigne, "De L'Amitié"

The dream's forfeit was a night in jail
and now the slant light is crepuscular.
Papers or not, you are a foreigner
whose name is always difficult to spell.
You pack your one valise. You ring the bell.
Might it not be prudent to disappear
beneath that mauve-blue sky above the square
fronting your cosmopolitan hotel?
You know two shortcuts to the train station
which could get you there, on foot, in time.
The person who's apprised of your intention
and seems to be your traveling companion
is merely the detritus of a dream.
You cross the lobby and go out alone.

You crossed the lobby and went out alone
through the square, where two red-headed girls played
hopscotch on a chalk grid, now in the shade,
of a broad-leafed plane tree, now in the sun.
The lively, lovely, widowed afternoon
disarmed, uncoupled, shuffled and disarrayed
itself; despite itself, dismayed
you with your certainties, your visa, gone
from your breast-pocket, or perhaps expired.
At the reception desk, no one inquired
if you'd be returning. Now you wonder why.
When the stout conductor comes down the aisle,

mustached, red-faced, at first jovial,
and asks for your passport, what will you say?

When they ask for your passport, will you say
that town's name they'd find unpronounceable
which resonates, when uttered, like a bell
in your mind's tower, as it did the day
you carried your green schoolbag down the gray
fog-cobbled street, past church, bakery, shul,
past farm women setting up market stalls
it was so early. "I am on my way
to school in _____." You were part of the town
now, not the furnished rooms you shared
with Mutti, since the others disappeared.
Your knees were red with cold; your itchy wool
socks had inched down, so you stooped to pull
them up, a student and a citizen.

You are a student and a citizen
of whatever state is transient.
You are no more or less the resident
of a hotel than you were of that town
whose borders were disputed and redrawn.
A prince conceded to a president.
Another language became relevant
to merchants on that street a child walked down
whom you remember, in the corridors
of cities you inhabit, polyglot
as the distinguished scholar you were not
to be. A slight accent sets you apart,
but it would mark you on that peddlers'-cart
street now. Which language, after all, is yours?

Which language, after all these streets, is yours,
and why are you here, waiting for a train?
You could have run a hot bath, read Montaigne.
But would footsteps beyond the bathroom door's
bolt have disturbed the nondescript interior's
familiarity, shadowed the plain
blue draperies? You reflect, you know no one
who would, of you, echo your author's
Because it was he; because it was I,
as a unique friendship's non sequitur.
No footsteps and no friend: that makes you free.
The train approaches, wreathed in smoke like fur
around the shoulders of a dowager
with no time for sentimentality.

With no time for sentimentality,
mulling a twice-postponed book review,
you take an empty seat. Opposite you
a voluble immigrant family
is already unwrapping garlicky
sausages—an unshaven man and his two
red-eared sons.
           You once wrote: it is true,
awful, and unimportant, finally,
that if the opportunity occurs
some of the exiles become storm-troopers;
and you try, culpably, to project these three
into some torch-lit future, filtering out
their wrangling (one of your languages) about
the next canto in their short odyssey.

The next canto in your short odyssey
will open, you know this, in yet another
hotel room. They have become your mother
country: benevolent anonymity
of rough starched sheets, dim lamp, rickety
escritoire, one window. Your neighbors gather
up their crusts and rinds. Out of a leather
satchel, the man takes their frayed identity
cards, examines them. The sons watch, pale
and less talkative. A border, passport control,
draw near: rubber stamp or interrogation?
You hope the customs officer lunched well;
reflect on the recurrent implication
of the dream's forfeit. One night in jail?

Canzone

Late afternoon, a work-table four stories
above the rain-slick January street
—and words begin to slide into a story
someone told once. Repeating well-known stories
with new inflections, does the teller add
a nuance or a chapter to the story—
the teller's own, or a recounted story—
so that it takes an unexpected turn
and doesn't, like a child from school, return
at the same time, to the same place? History
cycles over in place, unless we learn
something from the cycle—learn to unlearn

what's overdetermined. The child learns how to learn
from listening to, embroidering on stories
repeated to delight, to soothe. She learns
from delight, from repetition, learns
syntactic play, learns courtesies the street
exacts (accepts, rewards when they're well learned),
learns over time how much there's still to learn.
At eight, eighteen, you promise that you'll add
a word to your lexicon each day, add
a book to your bedside reading, start to learn
a language. Now, like a trip, you plan return-
ing to a book read once, think how you'll turn

that page down, give the writer one more turn
to teach what you were not prepared to learn
in adolescence, stubborn, taciturn
inclined to shut the book, mentally turn
on your heel, exit the uncongenial story

which did not give your idée fixe a turn
to play the diva. Less inclined to turn
on Flaubert, having walked down the street
Mme Moreau lived in, you know your street
is also paved with stories. If you could turn
doors and windows back like pages, had
a listener's wit, there'd be nothing to add.

But even a silent interlocutor adds
something to a narrative, which turns
in spirals, auricular labyrinths, to add
conjunction and conjecture. (The teller adds
specifics, so the listener will learn
extreme attention.) Remember how you had
smiled and hummed the line you knew on the ad
in the métro, history and a story
Clément wrote, Montand sang, and, one more history:
the passage from commune to commuter. Add
the station's name, a grassy path, a street
whose western limit is your own home street.

Life hums, a wire pulled taut between that street
and one across an ocean. Stretch back, add
East Fifth, East Sixth, East Tenth, Henry Street,
Perine Place, Natoma Street, Paddington Street.
In dream-labyrinth nights, I turn
a corner, one street becomes another street
in another country, yet on that street
doorway flows into hallway: no need to learn
my way; I know the way. Awake, I earn
the daily recognition of the streets
I live on, dual, counterpoint, their stories
enunciate a cautious history.

Now and from memory's clerestory,
my vision of that palimpsest, a street,
(as fading daylight, gold on velvet, adds
textured layer) turns outward as streetlights turn
on, lights cut out lives, limits: What can I learn?

Respite in a Minor Key

I would like an unending stretch of drizzly
weekday afternoons, in a moulting season:
nowhere else to go but across the street for
bread, and the paper.

Later, faces, voices across a table,
or an autumn fricassee, cèpes and shallots,
sipping Gigondas as I dice and hum to
Charpentier's vespers.

No one's waiting for me across an ocean.
What I can't understand or change is distant.
War is a debate, or at worst, a headlined
nightmare. But waking

it will be there still, and one morning closer
to my implication in what I never
chose, elected, as my natal sky rains down
civilian ashes.

Anyone

There was never a prelapsarian childhood
There was echoed death, the penuried silence of war,
a vague, appropriate deference to her betters.
She might have glimpsed the scrolls, she was not the one for
whom they had been saved, though she was saved, from the
    fire that struck by
night, or the slow attrition of day to day
death, to live the life of an unmarked citizen
whom only the close and quotidian might betray.
She was remunerated for her labors
which fed no refugees, stopped no battalions.
Uncertainly informed, she had opinions
that sometimes differed from those of her neighbors.
Reading alone the horrible headlines, when
there was public outrage, she would know private grief.
Her obituary would be vague and brief:
there was nothing to interest historians in her letters.

Morning News

Spring wafts up the smell of bus exhaust, of bread
and fried potatoes, tips green on the branches,
repeats old news: arrogance, ignorance, war.
A cinder-block wall shared by two houses
is new rubble. On one side was a kitchen
sink and a cupboard, on the other was
a bed, a bookshelf, three framed photographs.

Glass is shattered across the photographs;
two half-circles of hardened pocket bread
sit on the cupboard. There provisionally was
shelter, a plastic truck under the branches
of a fig tree. A knife flashed in the kitchen,
merely dicing garlic. Engines of war
move inexorably toward certain houses

while citizens sit safe in other houses
reading the newspaper, whose photographs
make sanitized excuses for the war.
There are innumerable kinds of bread
brought up from bakeries, baked in the kitchen:
the date, the latitude, tell which one was
dropped by a child beneath the bloodied branches.

The uncontrolled and multifurcate branches
of possibility infiltrate houses'
walls, windowframes, ceilings. Where there was
a tower, a town: ash and burnt wires, a graph
on a distant computer screen. Elsewhere, a kitchen
table's setting gapes, where children bred
to branch into new lives were culled for war.

Who wore this starched smocked cotton dress? Who wore
this jersey blazoned for the local branch
of the district soccer team? Who left this black bread
and this flat gold bread in their abandoned houses?
Whose father begged for mercy in the kitchen?
Whose memory will frame the photograph
and use the memory for what it was

never meant for by this girl, that old man, who was
caught on a ball field, near a window: war,
exhorted through the grief a photograph
revives. (Or was the team a covert branch
of a banned group; were maps drawn in the kitchen,
a bomb thrust in a hollowed loaf of bread?)
What did the old men pray for in their houses

of prayer, the teachers teach in schoolhouses
between blackouts and blasts, when each word was
flensed by new censure, books exchanged for bread,
both hostage to the happenstance of war?
Sometimes the only schoolroom is a kitchen.
Outside the window, black strokes on a graph
of broken glass, birds line up on bare branches.

"This letter curves, this one spreads its branches
like friends holding hands outside their houses."
Was the lesson stopped by gunfire? Was
there panic, silence? Does a torn photograph
still gather children in the teacher's kitchen?
Are they there meticulously learning war-
time lessons with the signs for house, book, bread?

Essay on Departure

And when you leave, and no one's left behind,
do you leave a cluttered room, a window framing
a zinc roof, other mansard windows? Do you
leave a row of sycamores, a river
that flows in your nocturnal pulse, a moon
sailing late-risen through clouds silvered by
the lights flung up from bridges? Do you leave
the wicker chairs the café owner stacks
at half-past-midnight while the last small clutch
of two girls and a boy smoke and discuss
what twenty-year-olds in cafés discuss
past midnight, with no war on here? You leave
the one and then the other, the all-night
eight-aisles-of-sundries with a pharmacy
cloned six times in one mile on upper Broadway.
Everywhere you're leaving something, leaving
no one, leaving as a season fades,
leaving the crisp anticipation of
the new, before its gold drops on the rain-
slick crossings to the walkways over bridges,
the schoolyard's newly painted porte-cochère:
remembered details. You're no longer there.
What's left when you have left, when what is left is
coins on the table and an empty cup?
An August lapse begins; the shutters drop
and lock, whatever follows is conjecture.
The sound feels final, punitive, a trap
shutting its jaws, though when the selfsame structure
was rolled up mornings, it was hopeful noise,
a reprieve from insomnia, a day's

presence opening possibility.
As you leave the place, you bring the time
you spent there to a closed parenthesis.
Now it is part of that amorphous past
parceled into flashes, slide-vignettes.
You'll never know if just what you forget's
the numinous and right detail, the key—
but to a door that is no longer yours,
glimpse of a morning-lit interior's
awakening silhouette, with the good blue
sky reflected on the tall blue walls,
then shadow swallows what was/wasn't true,
shutters the windows, sheathes the shelves in dust,
retains a sour taste and discards the kiss,
clings to the mood stripped of its narrative.
You take the present tense along. The place
you're leaving stops, dissolves into a past
in which it may have been, or it may not
have been (corroborate, but it's still gone)
the place you were, the moment that you leave.